15 WALKS FROM BU
WASDALE & ESKDALE

PAUL BUTTLE

Published by

᚛ᚋᚐᚇᚑᚱᚅ

I would like to thank Jonathan Miller for the great help he has given in preparing this guide and also Hilary Drummond and once more Pádraig Ciobháin for his useful few words.

First published July, 1994

Reprinted February 1998, March 2001, May 2004

ISBN 0 9513717 8 9

© P. Buttle 1994.

Published by Amadorn, 18 Brewery Lane, Keswick, Cumbria.

Typeset in Palatino by An Údar, 18 Greta Villas, Keswick, Cumbria.

Printed by Nuffield Press, Abingdon.

CONTENTS

INTRODUCTION

The walks in this guide cover the western fells of the Lake District and are centred on three of its most impressive valleys. Six walks are centred around the Buttermere/Crummock Water valley, four around Wasdale and five around Eskdale. There are four valley walks, one moorland ramble and the rest are all fell walks. I would venture to say that at least two thirds of the walks have some originality in that they use some way of approach that is not commonly used which greatly improves them and which I hope will justify the price of this guide.

How the walks are ordered.

The walks are grouped in three categories; Valley Walks, Intermediate Walks and High Level Fell Walks. Within these categories I've tried to order the walks by the amount of effort that is required to complete them. So in general as you go through the guide the harder the walks become. That at least is the theory and the explanation for how the walks have been set out.

Suggested Times.

Each walk has a suggested time which should be regarded simply as a rule of thumb. I've calculated these times by allowing for a generous hour for every thousand feet of ascent and an hour for every three miles. It should not be too difficult to do any of the walks in a time less than the one suggested. On the other hand if you take a more leisurely approach to the task you might find the walks take you longer. Only practical investigation will establish which.

What map to use?

On the valley walks I would like to think that the directional notes and sketch maps are sufficient for the walks to be accomplished without the need of a map. But for all the other walks a map is really essential. For which purpose there are three types of Ordnance Survey Maps that can be considered:

The 'One Inch' Tourist Map of the Lake District. Scale 1: 63,360.
This map covers all the walks in this guide and indeed all the rest of the fells in the Lake District. One inch on the map represents a mile on the ground. Although for me this is the map's great virtue I now find the present edition too painful to look at. It is now printed on thin paper, is covered with purple splodges and even has other things printed on the back of it! But worse of all, an act of pure desecration, the contours on it have been metricated. In a previous guide I asked how many people were there that visualised distances in miles but heights in metres? Perhaps there are more than I thought for I write these words on the day of the official inauguration of the Channel Tunnel and in this morning's edition of *The Independent* there is a diagram of the tunnel showing the length of it in miles and the depth of it in metres! If like me however you think entirely in imperial measurements it is worth getting a pre-metricated edition of this map if you possibly can.

Landranger Series Sheet 89. Scale 1:50,000
This covers all the walks in this guide except for one mile of the Harter Fell and Hard Knott walk, which is on sheet 96. Although only a slightly larger scale than the 'One Inch' map it is surprisingly clearer. On the other hand it is a completely metricated map. I still haven't got used to measuring map distances in inch and a quarters to work out mileages. For anyone nurtured on the metric system however the comparable task is much simpler; every two centimetres on the map represents a single kilometre.

Outdoor Leisure Map English Lakes : Scale 1:25,500
These are incredibly detailed maps and the best maps of the Lake District though they are of course a more expensive option. There are four that cover the Lake District. Two of them cover the walks in this guide; the North Western sheet and the South Western sheet. There is one draw back to these maps however; rights of way are represented with bold green dashed lines which is fine when they represent footpaths but not so fine when they don't. Sometimes, quite often in fact, there may not actually be a path following a right of way and this can lead to no little confusion. Be careful using these maps to notice the very faint black dashed lines on them which represent actual existing paths, sometimes these can be very distinct paths, it is often the case that it will be these paths you are following rather than the bolder green rights of way.

Public Transport.

Unfortunately there is very little public transport in the Western Lakes. At the time of writing I am only aware of the Mountain Goat minibus which runs from Keswick to Buttermere in the summer and the Eskdale miniature railway that runs from Ravenglass to Boot. What transport there is is always changing. Anyone wishing to find further information on this subject would do best to telephone an information service operated by Cumbria County Council called 'Travel Link', on Carlisle (01228) 606000.

Safety on the Fells.

Most of the walks in this guide are serious fell walks and cover the most precipitous parts of the Lake District, ensure therefore that you are properly equipped to venture on them. Conditions on the fells can sometimes change very quickly.

Tá na foclaibh seo scríte anso d'fhonn an spás
a líonadh a bheadh ann á n-éagmais

BUTTERMERE LAKE

Distance	4 1/2 miles
Total Feet of Ascent	200 feet
Suggested Time	2 hours
Starting Point	Buttermere village car park (NY 175 169)

This walk is probably the most attractive level walk in the Lake District. It hardly needs any directions as it is so straightforward, apart from suggesting that the walk should be done clockwise round the lake. The reason for this is simple enough; the best views are to be had looking up the valley which can't be seen so well from the south-western shoreline of the lake as much of it is thickly wooded with conifer trees. The great majority of people who walk round the lake however tend to do so anti-clockwise, so be prepared to receive several salutations.

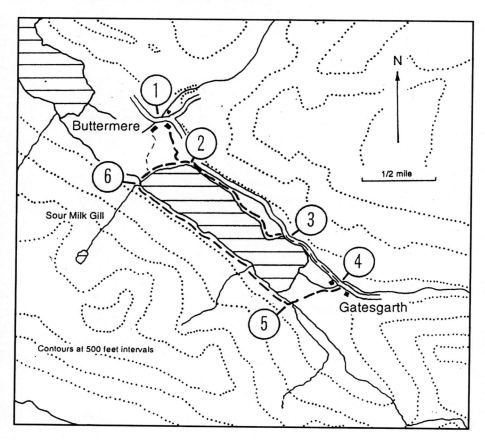

1 Beginning from the Bridge Hotel turn right to follow the main road for fifty yards and turn right in to the farmyard of Syke Farm which is signposted as being a bridleway leading to the lakeshore. The path begins from the end of the farmyard and leads to the northern corner of the lake. (1/2 mile)

2 The path is so distinct there is no problem following it here on. Where however it links back on to the B5289, as you will probably notice, there is a permissive path which continues a little further along the lake shore before itself linking up with the B5289. (1 1/4 miles)

3 Unfortunately it is now necessary to continue along the roadway as far as Gatesgarth farm where, next to a post box, is to be found the start of an indicated bridleway back to Buttermere, initially following the side of Gatesgarthdale Beck. (1/4 mile)

4 Within a hundred yards the path links on to a trackway leading from the farmyard which almost immediately branches in two. Follow the right hand branch which leads to a wooden bridge crossing Warnscale Beck across which is a five bar gate and kissing gate. (1/2 mile)

5 After passing through the gate turn immediately right on to a signposted public bridleway leading back to Buttermere village. Entering a conifer wood the path branches in two but within a few hundred yards the two paths merge back together. Reaching the western corner of the lake the path crosses the foot of Sour Milk Gill and then swings round to the right to a footbridge crossing the lake's outflow. (1 1/2 miles)

6 From the bridge a distinct track leads back to Buttermere village, but by turning right it is possible to continue along a permissive path which follows the northern shore of the lake and links back on to the path you started on. (3/4 mile)

ESKDALE

Distance	6 $\frac{1}{2}$ miles
Total Feet of Ascent	Negligible
Suggested Time	2 $\frac{1}{2}$ hours
Starting Point	Boot (NY 177 010)
Car Parking	At the Burnmoor Inn with landlord's permission.

Eskdale is a wonderful valley of snug farmsteads and small deciduous woods bounded by rugged fells. The rock in the valley has a slightly pinkish colour which gives the houses and even the field boundary walls a warm look. The walk essentially follows the course of the river Esk, after which the valley is named, upstream to the foot of Hardknott Pass and then returns by way of the valley's main road. This is a pleasant lane to walk along when free of traffic which unfortunately is not its usual condition in high summer.

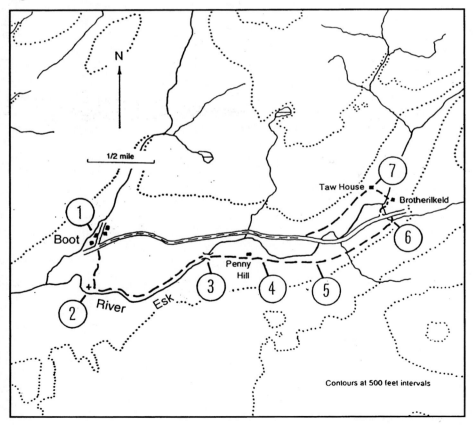

1 From the Burnmoor Inn walk back to the main valley road. Walk straight across the road on to a lane signposted as leading to the valley church. The lane leads to the river Esk on the banks of which the church is situated. (1/2 mile)

2 Here turn left and follow the pathway leading initially along the river bank. This is a distinct path which more or less parallels the river Esk until it reaches a stone bridge spanning the river. (1 mile)

3 Cross over the bridge and follow the farm access road that leads directly from it to Penny Hill Farm. A right of way, a bridleway, continues past the farm and is way-marked with a series of blue arrows that indicate that it follows a rough trackway. About two hundred yards from the farm the trackway branches in two. (1/2 mile)

4 Bear left, still following the blue arrow waymarks. Passing through a gateway the track becomes little more than a line of ruts until it follows the outer side of a field boundary wall. Soon after crossing a small beck the bridleway reaches a signpost at the edge of a wood. (1/2 mile)

5 From here chose the path which the signpost indicates as leading to Hardknott. This path follows the outer edge of the wood's boundary wall then moves on to a foot-bridge crossing the next beck, a hundred yards ahead, and then through a gateway, but not over the stile immediately to the left of the gate. The path continues through some woodland and then along the foot of some open fell and eventually joins an old bridleway which after passing through two kissing gates and over a stone footbridge joins the Hardknott Pass road. (3/4 mile)

6 Here turn left. Just over a hundred yards along the road turn right on to the farm access road to Brotherilkeld farm. Just before entering the farmyard bear left on to a footpath which follows the banks of the river Esk which soon leads to a footbridge spanning the river. From the other side of the bridge an enclosed path leads to Taw House Farm. (1/2 mile)

7 From Taw House Farm follow the farm's access road back to the main valley road. On reaching the road turn right and follow the road back to Boot. (2 1/2 miles)

THE LOWESWATER CIRCUIT

Distance	7 miles
Total Feet of Ascent	400 feet
Suggested Time	2 1/2 hours
Starting Point	Scale Bridge car park (NY 149 214)

The area immediately around Loweswater lake is very gentle and pastoral yet it is also
set in the midst of some very rugged and imposing mountain scenery. Indeed the view
looking down the length of Crummock Water in to the depth of the Buttermere valley
and on to Great Gable, which is perhaps seen to its best advantage along the first mile
of the walk, is one of the most impressive valley views in the Lake District. There are
also two points on this walk where it is possible to enjoy a very civilised break for
refreshments. Firstly at he Grange Country House Hotel which serves bar meals and
teas. Its spacious lawn, where one can sit, has a quintessential Lakeland view of unbe-
lievable beauty and yet the hotel itself lies just outside the national park. And secondly
at the Kirkstile Inn, which caters well for hungry and or thirsty walkers of all tastes, be
they abstemious or non-abstemious.

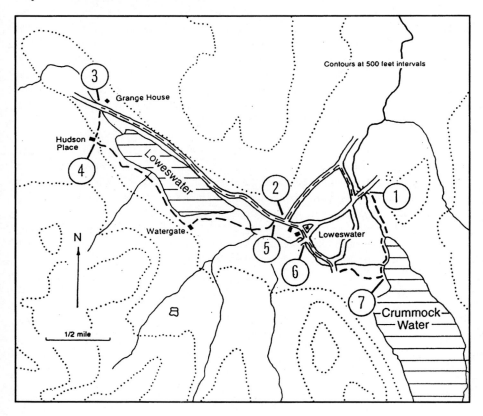

1 From the car park turn left across Scalehill Bridge and take the first turn right on to a road signposted as leading to Thackthwaite. The road soon comes to a junction. Here turn left. Within three quarters of a mile this road also comes to a junction. (1 1/4 miles)

2 Here turn right. The road soon comes to follow the north-eastern lakeshore of Loweswater. For a few hundred yards along the lakeshore there is an alternative lakeshore path one can use, but it runs through such a thick growth of bushes and saplings there is little advantage in using it. Eventually the road comes to The Grange Country House Hotel. (1 3/4 miles)

3 Immediately opposite the driveway of the Grange Country House Hotel is the start of a driveway leading to Hudson Place Farm also signposted as being a bridleway to Holme Wood and Fangs Brow. Follow the driveway. As it curves right in to the farm-yard of Hudson Place a trackway veers from it off to the left. A slate sign claims it is also a footpath. (1/4 mile)

4 It is in fact a bridleway and for much of its length is also a broad motorable trackway which parallels or follows the south-west shoreline of Loweswater and then passes through Watergate Farm, from where it leads back up to the Loweswater and Mockerkin road, becoming itself in its final few hundred yards a surfaced road. (1 3/4 miles)

5 On reaching the roadway turn right. A few hundred yards on take the first turn right. Where the road curves left around Loweswater church branch right, past the Kirkstile Inn, on to a road indicated by a sign saying "No Road to the Lake". (1/4 mile)

6 Continue along the road signed as not leading to the Lake and take the first turn right on to a road which is indicated as being a cul-de-sac. Within two hundred yards a signpost indicates a footpath leading off from the road to the left to the north-west corner of Crummock Water. The final stage of the path runs through an exceptionally soggy field, and in the final hundred yards of it you will need to cross a stile spanning a wire fence that encloses the field and then follow a line of conifer trees to the water's edge. (3/4 mile)

7 Along the water's edge a path runs northwards along the top of a low concrete wall retaining the waters of the lake to its northern tip, where it crosses two footbridges spanning the lake's divided outflow. Within a hundred yards of these twin bridges a broad pathway leads northwards, away from the lake, back to the walk's starting point. (3/4 mile)

THE CRUMMOCK WATER CIRCUIT

Distance	8 $\frac{1}{2}$ miles
Total Feet of Ascent	700 feet
Suggested Time	4 hours
Starting Point	Buttermere village car park (NY 174 169)

Few people seem to walk the complete circuit of Crummock Water, certainly nowhere near the numbers who walk round Buttermere, maybe this is because it is thought the circuit requires too much road walking along the busy B5289. In fact it is possible to restrict such road walking to little more than half a mile. There are some striking views on the circuit, either towards Grasmoor or along the length of the lake towards the head of the Buttermere valley. In addition there is also the possibility of calling in to a pub half way round.

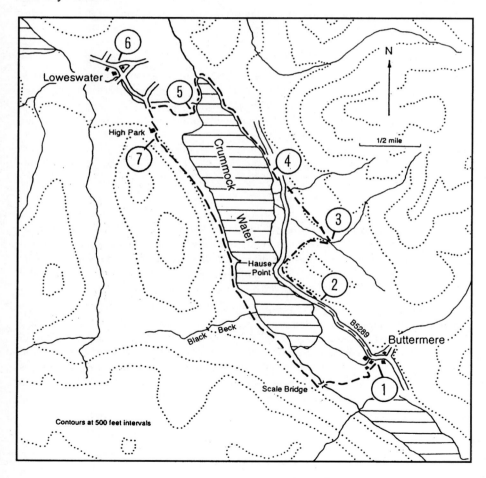

1 Starting from the village of Buttermere begin walking northwards along the B5289. About a hundred yards before the B5289 comes to follow the lakeshore of Crummock Water veering off to the right, indicated with a small wooden signpost, is the start of a grassy bridleway. (3/4 mile)

2 It is my own guess that this humble path was once the main route in to the valley before a road was forged around Hause Point, the protruding crag that juts in to the lake over which the path crosses. Descending the other side of the crag the path rejoins the road. Walk fifty yards along the road and branch right on to a signposted footpath following the outer side of a boundary wall. The path soon comes to a footbridge crossing Rannerdale Beck. (1 mile)

3 Cross over the bridge and turn left to follow a path leading back towards the lake to rejoin the B5289. Continue northwards along the road a few hundred yards and pass through a kissing gate on the left hand side of the road giving access to Fletcher Fields. From the gate a path leads down to the lakeshore of Crummock Water. (3/4 mile)

4 The path continues as a lakeshore path around the northern end of Crummock Water. The north-western part of the lake has a low concrete retaining wall. Where this wall concludes the path crosses a wooden stile which spans a wire fence. (1 1/2 miles)

5 At this point you can, of course, continue following the lakeshore, but if you wish to visit the hamlet of Loweswater and the Kirkstile Inn at this point turn right and follow the fence you have just crossed. A few yards along the fence is a second stile. After crossing this second stile turn left. A narrow path winds through a field of soggy vegetation to a third stile. After the third stile the path is more distinct. A fourth stile and then a gate follows and the path arrives at the terminus of a surfaced road. Turn right. The road soon comes to a junction. Here turn left to reach the hamlet of Loweswater. (3/4 mile)

6 To return to the lakeshore retrace your steps to the point where you joined the roadway. Here instead of turning left on to the path you formerly followed continue straight ahead along a trackway leading past High Park Farm. As you pass the end of the garden at the back of the former farmhouse look up to your right. Set in the field's boundary wall up to your right is a stone stile with a sign indicating that it is the start of a path to Crummock Water. (1/2 mile)

7 This path gradually descends to the lakeshore where it merges with the lakeshore path. Approaching Black Beck the path branches in two. Even though the right hand branch crosses a footbridge it is the left hand branch which is easiest to follow. Within a short distance this path merges with a much bolder path coming from Scale Force, and within half a mile of this point the path comes to Scale Bridge. Leading from the bridge is a broad trackway which leads back to Buttermere village. (3 1/4 miles)

BURNMOOR TARN

Distance	6 ³/₄ miles
Total Feet of Ascent	800 feet
Suggested Time	3 hours
Starting Point	Woolpack Inn (NY 190 009)
Car Parking	Inn car park with landlord's permission

This is a simple easy walk across some wonderful, open, sweeping landscape to the largest tarn in the Lake District. Overlooking the tarn is Burnmoor Lodge one of the most isolated buildings in the national park. The descent back to Eskdale is a delight as it affords some very attractive views of this very pleasing dale. To conclude with there is a river side walk back to the starting point. All in all the walk is a good insight in to the valley's many attractions.

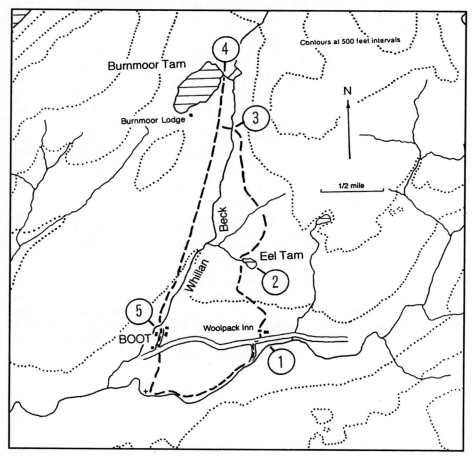

1 Walk round the left hand side of the hotel. At the back of the hotel, starting from a flight of steps and marked with a white cross, is the start of the path. After a steep pull of around five hundred feet, through some rugged terrain, the path reaches Eel Tarn. (3/4 mile)

2 After moving round the far side of the tarn the path twice branches in two within the space of a few hundred yards. These branchings, however, are hardly perceptible. On a clear day you will see a path stretching ahead of you in a northerly direction, the same direction as you approach the tarn, this is the path you should follow, ignoring the first branch to the right and the second to the left, if you do notice them. The northerly path eventually reaches a broad wooden foot bridge, Lambford Bridge, spanning Whillan Beck. (1 1/4 miles)

3 From the other side of the bridge there is no evident path to follow. Simply climb directly uphill. After climbing a hundred yards or so there is the vague semblance of a path but it is uncairned. Ignore this and press another hundred yards uphill in which distance you should locate a broader path which is also well cairned. This is the 'Old Corpse Road', an old bridleway that links Eskdale with Wasdale. Here turn right and follow the path to Bulatt Bridge which spans the outflow from Burnmoor Tarn, Whillan Beck again. (1/2 mile)

4 From Bulatt Bridge turn around and follow the Old Corpse Road south. After crossing open ground the path passes through a gate in to an enclosed field. Shortly after passing through a second gate it may seem as if the route veers left through a third gate to move sharply downhill towards Whillan Beck. In fact the third gate you should pass through is directly ahead at this point, as the Corpse Road continues its more or less direct line to the village of Boot. (2 1/4 miles)

5 Walk through the village to join the main valley road. *(Here you have the option of simply turning left and following the road back to the Woolpack Inn [1 mile]. Alternatively if you wish to keep road walking to a minimum....)* Here cross the road on to the unsurfaced lane which is signposted as leading to the valley church. This will bring you to the river Esk on the banks of which the church is situated. Here turn left and follow the pathway which initially follows the river bank. This is a distinct path which eventually reaches a stone bridge, Doctor Bridge. Do not cross the bridge but follow the road that leads to it. This soon joins the main valley road. A few hundred yards to the right is the walk's starting point, the Woolpack Inn. Time for sustenance! (3/4 mile)

MELLBREAK 1668 feet

Distance	4 3/4 miles
Total Feet of Ascent	1500 feet
Suggested Time	3 hours
Starting Point	Kirkstile Inn, Loweswater. (NY 142 209)
Car parking	Verge side parking possible by phone box.

Mellbreak is only a modest sized fell by Lakeland standards though it looks very impressive due of the steepness of its slopes, especially when seen from Loweswater. Because of the steepness of those slopes its ascent is somewhat demanding despite its lack of height. Its great virtue as a fell are the views that are to be had from it. There are some striking views of the Crummock Water and Buttermere valley to be had from Mellbreak, especially from its southern top, probably the best views to be had in this part of the Lake District. The return route is via Mosedale which is very empty and quiet. So although this is a fell walk of very modest proportions it is very worthwhile accomplishing.

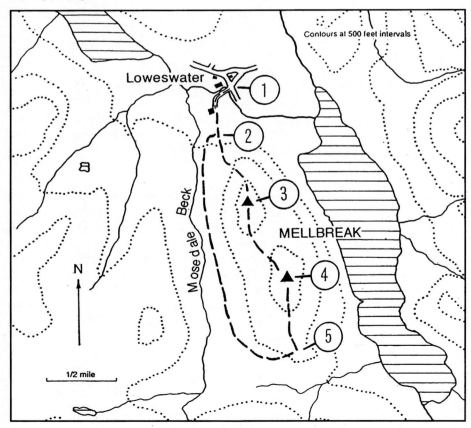

1   Beginning from the Kirkstile Inn follow the road which the pub overlooks and is sign-posted as being a 'No Through Road'. Passing through a farmyard the road becomes a rough trackway. After passing through a six bar gate the track swings right but direct-ly ahead a path climbs uphill through a break in a small copse of conifer trees. ($1/2$ mile)

2   Emerging from the copse the path is not immediately evident but by continuing the line of the path directly uphill within a few yards a path becomes again evident. The path pulls up to the base of a scree shoot which it then proceeds to climb in a series of zig-zags to the base of a gully from which the scree emanates. As an easier alternative to ascending the gully look for a narrow path that moves away to the right from the base and then ascends to the top of the gully in one large zig-zag. From the top of the gully a distinct path leads to the first summit of Mellbreak. ($1/2$ mile)

3   From this first summit a distinct path leads to the second summit along the broad ridge of the fell. Midway between these two summits the path branches in two. Follow the left hand path to the second summit. $3/4$ mile)

4   From this second summit a very grassy path leads downhill in the direction of Scale Force a ravine on the slopes of Red Pike, the fell which is seen when looking south-east. At a point where the steep gradient of the path relents and becomes almost level be careful to note that at this point the path intersects with another grassy path. ($1/2$ mile)

5   Here turn right on to this new path which moves around the base of Mellbreak, becoming increasingly distinctive as it does so. Eventually the substantialness of the path rises to that of a trackway the later part of which was used at the start of the walk and which now serves as the concluding part of the walk. (2 $1/2$ miles)

FLEETWITH PIKE 2126 feet
& HAY STACKS 1900 feet

Distance	4 1/2 miles
Total Feet of Ascent	2400 feet
Suggested Time	4 hours
Starting Point	Gatesgarth car park (NY 196 150)

This walk can be considered as being a more modest alternative to the Buttermere Fells walk described on page 34, though it is also a very worthy walk in its own right. It covers some very rugged terrain and has some splendid views particularly of Buttermere and Crummock Water. The initial climb to the top of Fleetwith is long and steep. There are three or four occasions on this climb where you might think you are about to reach the top only to find it is just a change of gradient you have come to. Hay Stacks has become an extremely popular fell possibly because of the way Wainwright extolled its virtues. It is on Hay Stacks, by the side of Innominate Tarn, that Wainwright's ashes are now scattered.

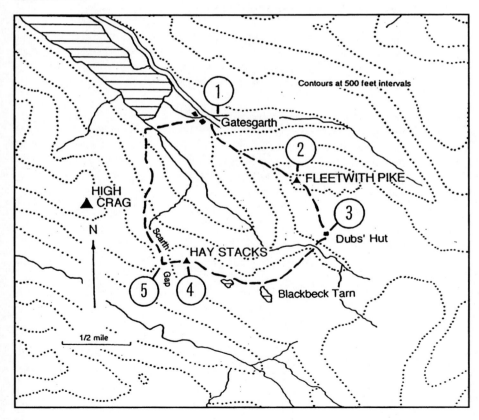

1 From the car park follow the road uphill for roughly a hundred yards and turn right on to a trackway signposted as being a bridleway. Walk ten yards along this track and turn immediately left on to a pathway that has practically no discernibility to begin with but is clear enough further on as it zig-zags uphill to the left of a white cross. There follows a long steep climb of 1700 feet to the top of Fleetwith Pike. (1 mile)

2 From the summit cairn the path continues eastwards along the crest of Fleetwith's summit ridge. But veering off to your right from the summit cairn is a much thinner path leading towards the quarry wastes of Dubs' Quarry. Nearing the quarry the path becomes ill defined and you will probably have to make your own line of descent. You should however have no difficulty in locating Dubs' Hut in the middle of the quarry wastes, originally a quarrymen's refuge, latterly a climber's hut and presently an incipient ruin. ($1/2$ mile)

3 From the hut a path leads downhill to Warnscale Beck. On the other side of the beck the path becomes very worn, so worn indeed there is little chance of losing it. It leads past Blackbeck Tarn and Innominate Tarn and on to the top of Hay Stacks. (1 mile)

4 The summit of Hay Stacks consists of two rocky, parallel ridges with a narrow, elongated, little tarn in between. It is from the second of these ridges, the lower one, beginning from a metal post that a steep rocky path descends to Scarf Gap, the gap between Hay Stacks and High Crag. ($1/4$ mile)

5 Running across Scarf Gap is an old packhorse route. Here turn right and follow the route downhill towards Buttermere lake. In the final part of the descent the path follows the edge of a small copse of trees. At the corner of this copse the path turns sharp right and follows the lower boundary of the copse and finally reaches a five bar gate at the foot of the descent. From the gate a broad trackway leads back to Gatesgarth farm and the walk's starting point. (1 $1/2$ mile)

GRASMOOR 2791 feet

Distance	8 1/4 miles
Total Feet of Ascent	2400 feet
Suggested Time	5 1/2 hours
Starting Point	Cinderdale Beck Car Park, 600 yards north of Rannerdale Farm (NY 162 194)

This walk involves a very steep ascent though the top of Grasmoor itself is very flat, or at least it gives that illusion. Coming to the summit of the fell one gains a very dramatic view looking down on to Crummock Water and the route of one's ascent. The descent is via Gasgale Gill which flows through what is probably the narrowest valley in the Lake District whose valley floor has little room for anything else but the gill itself, which means there are one or two awkward steps when following its course. Heather clad it is an intriguing valley and quite distinct from any other in the Lake District.

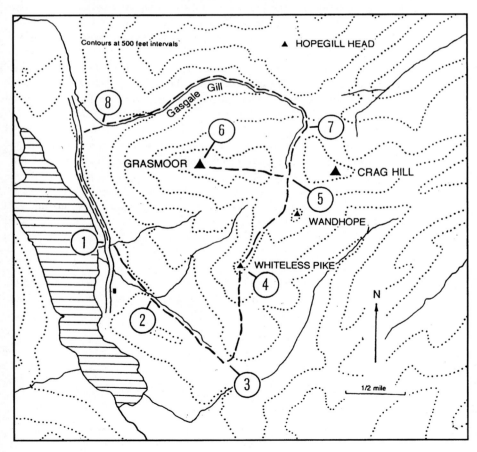

1 Beginning from the end of Cinderdale Beck car park is the start of a trackway that leads in to Rannerdale which eventually comes to a footbridge crossing Rannerdale Beck. ($1/2$ mile)

2 Cross over the footbridge and over a stile immediately opposite. Once over the stile turn left on to a footpath which continues up the valley eventually coming to a small saddle between Low Bank and Whiteless Breast where it meets a path climbing up from Buttermere to Whiteless Pike. (1 mile)

3 Here turn left and follow the new path uphill to the top of Whiteless Pike. ($3/4$ mile)

4 From the top of Whiteless Pike the path continues along Whiteless Edge and on to the shoulder of Wandope Moss, spot height 2406 feet. Here the path becomes relatively level and veers a little off to the left towards the gap between Grasmoor and Crag Hill where it intersects with a path running between these two hills. (1 mile)

5 Here turn left and follow this new path to the summit of Grasmoor which is marked with a stone shelter. ($3/4$ mile)

6 From the summit of Grasmoor return back to the col between Grasmoor and Crag Hill to the point you were at previously where the two paths intersect. Here turn left and follow your previous path down the other side of the col. The path soon starts to follow the head waters of Gasgale Gill. Nearing Coledale Hause, the gap between Hopegill Head and Crag Hill, the path veers away from the gill to the right towards the head of the Coledale valley. (1 $1/4$ miles)

7 Be careful at this point to locate a narrower path that branches left from the main path in order to continue following the course of Gasgale Gill. To confuse matters this path soon splits in two. Keep to the left branch which stays closest to the gill. The gill soon swings left and begins its long descent into the Gasgale valley eventually reaching a footbridge. (1 $3/4$ miles)

8 Crossing the footbridge the path becomes indistinct, however the B5289 is now only a few hundred yards away across easy open fell land. On reaching the road turn left to follow it back to your starting point. (1 $1/4$ miles)

WHIN RIGG 1755 feet
& ILLGILL HEAD 1978 feet

Distance	10 $\frac{1}{2}$ miles
Total Feet of Ascent	2000 feet
Suggested Time	5 $\frac{1}{2}$ hours
Starting Point	Where the Wasdale road joins the southern lake shore of Wastwater (NY 147 048)
Car Parking	Verge side parking along the lake shore.

The Wasdale Screes, a one thousand feet and more wall of scree that tumbles down into the waters of Wastwater, is one of the most striking views in the Lake District. At the top of the Screes Whin Rigg and Illgill Head form a broad undulating ridge with views towards England's highest peaks. The ascent is steep but comfortable and the walk along the ridge is easy. What is decidedly uncomfortable is the return walk along the shoreline of Wastwater along the base of the Screes. To a large extent this is all boulder hopping and should be done for the adventure of it. Do not attempt this path if you want an easy life. An easier alternative is of course to walk along the road way.

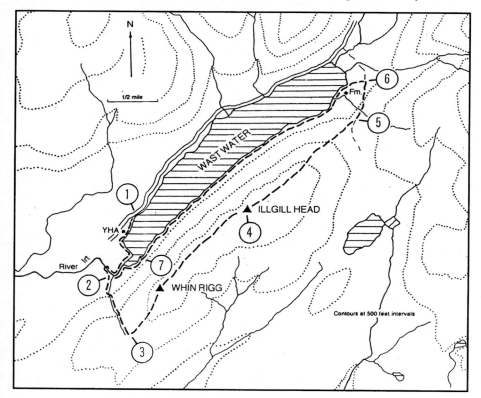

1 Starting from the single chevron sign which indicates where the road turns right away from the lake walk ten yards towards the southern end of the lake. You will soon notice a wall leading to the water's edge. Set in the wall is a wooden stile leading from which is a lake shore path. Follow this path to the lake's outflow, the river Irt, and continue following the river down stream to a stone bridge called Lund Bridge. Cross over the bridge and now follow the river up stream. Roughly two hundred and fifty yards from the bridge the path passes through a kissing gate set in a stone wall. Ten yards on from the kissing gate is the fairly inconspicuous start of a path that climbs uphill following the wall you have just past through. (1 1/4 miles)

2 The path leads to a trackway across which is a stile and five bar gate. Cross the stile and follow the right hand boundary of the field this gives access to. At the head of the field are two stiles either side of Greathall Gill which flows in to its top corner. Cross over either stile and continue along the path which follows the left hand side of the gill. At the top of a steep climb the path joins a distinct ridge path. (3/4 mile)

3 Here turn left. The path follows the ridge over Whin Rigg and on to Illgill Head. (1 3/4 miles)

4 From Illgill Head the path continues as a descent path to Wasdale Head in its later stages criss crossing a dilapidated wall to finally link with the Old Corpse Road that crosses from Wasdale to Eskdale; a much broader constructed path. (1 1/2 miles)

5 Here turn left and follow the path downhill. Where the path reaches almost level ground and crosses a small stream immediately to your left is a five bar gate giving access to a trackway leading to the lake shore. (1/2 mile)

6 *(If you wish to avoid using the path at the foot of the Screes continue on the Old Corpse Road path to the valley road which you can then follow back to the starting point. Otherwise....)* Follow the trackway to the lakeshore on reaching which it joins an access track to Wasdale Head Hall Farm. Here turn left. Where the track turns left in to the farm notice to your right a stile with a sign saying 'Footpath Lakeshore'. Continue on the footpath leading from the stile. This begins as a fairly broad path but quickly becomes fairly rocky. After a long stretch of boulder hopping the path eventually comes to the Wastwater pumping station. (3 1/4 miles)

7 Continue along the trackway leading from the station but after passing through a metal gate veer right on to a path keeping to the river's edge. This is the path which you set out on. Conclude the walk by retracing your earlier steps. (1 1/2 miles)

HARTER FELL 2140 feet
& HARD KNOTT 1803 feet

Distance	9 $\frac{1}{2}$ miles
Total Feet of Ascent	2500 feet
Suggested Time	5 $\frac{1}{2}$ hours
Starting Point	Lay-by above Wha House Farm (NY 202 009)

This walk affords some wonderful views of the upper Esk valley into the heart of the wildest mountain scenery in England, indeed the view of the Scafells from Hard Knott is one of Lakeland's finest views. The walk begins by actually walking away from the day's object, in order to obtain a more interesting approach from Penny Hill farm.

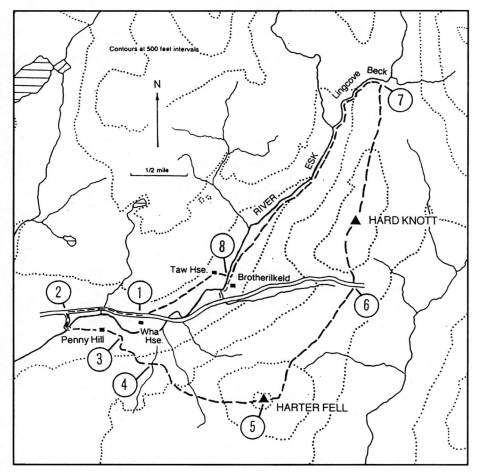

1   Walk along the road westwards, past the Woolpack, and take the first turn left on to a narrow access road to Penny Hill Farm. (3/4 mile)

2   After crossing a stone bridge the road branches in to two trackways. Follow the left hand track to Penny Hill Farm. From the farmyard a blue arrow waymark indicates that the right of way continues from the yard along an enclosed trackway. Roughly a hundred yards from the farm the track splits in two. Keep to the left hand more distinctive path. Within another hundred yards the track divides again. This time, as a miniature signpost indicates, it is the right hand track you should take to reach Harter Fell. (1/2 mile)

3   About a quarter of a mile on, and after a few hundred feet of climbing, a small sign post indicates the route to Harter Fell now leaves the distinct path you are on and follows the outer side of the boundary wall to your left. Only as you approach the wall will a path become evident. About another quarter mile on the path branches from the wall and crosses a small beck. (3/4 mile)

4   Notice at this point a path which follows the beck but ignore this path and instead aim for a small waymark post directly ahead which marks the start of a steep climb through the overlooking crags. From the top of this climb a short distance of level walking brings you to Spothow Gill bounded by a wire fence. From a stile in the fence a distinct path leads directly to the top of the fell, but not to the summit which is atop of a summit crag. Before scrambling up to the summit be sure to locate the path's highest point. (1 mile)

5   Resume following the path of ascent which in moving from its highest point now becomes a path of descent down the other side of the fell. Roughly fifty yards from the start of the descent it branches in two. It is important not to miss this. It is the left hand branch you should follow. (The right hand branch, the more direct one, descends down to Duddon.) The left hand path is quite grassy and needs some concentration to follow. Eventually it follows the upper boundary fence of the conifer forest occupying the Duddon valley and then heads for Hard Knott Pass, the final few hundred yards being more than a little vague. (1 1/4 miles)

6   From the summit of Hard Knott Pass a grassy path, none too obvious to begin with, ascends to the top of Hard Knott itself. From the top of Hard Knott head in a northerly direction. This initially is a very rocky and broken ridge and then becomes very rounded and grassy. There is something of a path along it but it is none too clear and easy to loose or confuse with sheep trods. The best approach is to keep to the crest of the ridge as much as possible using what path there is when there is one to be found. As you reach the end of the ridge veer left to join the path following Lingcove Beck. (2 miles)

7   Follow the path down stream. Reaching Lingcove Bridge it joins a path following the river Esk which likewise you should follow down stream. Drawing level with Brotherilkeld Farm the path comes to a narrow single beam footbridge spanning the river Esk. (2 1/2 miles)

8   Here cross the footbridge to Taw House Farm on the other side of the river and continue thence along the farm's access road. On joining the roadway the walk's starting point is just a few hundred yards to the right. (1 mile)

GREAT GABLE 2949 feet
& KIRK FELL 2630 feet

Distance	7 $^1/_2$ miles
Total Feet of Ascent	3500 feet
Suggested Time	6 hours
Starting Point	Wasdale Head car park (NY 187 087)

Great Gable is probably the most striking mountain in the Lake District. It looks impressive from every viewpoint especially from Wasdale. It is the outline of this view from Wasdale which is the emblem of the Lake District National Park. Included in this walk is Kirk Fell. This is a much less frequented summit than Gable, unjustly so for its broad rambling top is a pleasure to saunter over and there are also some striking views of Gable to be had from it as well. Crossing over Kirk Fell also makes it possible to descend to Wasdale via the old packhorse route crossing over Black Sail Pass which is a comfortable way of descent through the impressive valley of Mosedale.

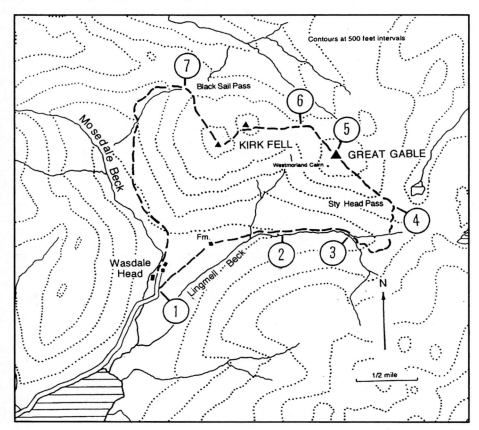

1 From the car park follow the trackway signposted as being a public bridleway to Sty Head Pass. After passing through Burnthwaite Farm the track becomes a stony pathway. Roughly half a mile from the farm the path crosses a footbridge. A quarter of a mile on from this it branches in two. (1 1/4 miles)

2 The left hand branch is the more obvious path but it is the right hand path which is the original bridleway and makes for a more interesting ascent, though both paths arrive at the same point. The right hand path follows the course of Lingmell Beck until it reaches a point where it crosses the river. The crossing point is denoted by a small cairn atop of a smooth boulder by the river's edge and another on the opposite bank. (1/2 mile)

3 From here on the path takes a zig-zagged course uphill. Nearing the top of the pass however the path comes back to the head waters of Lingmell Beck, Spouthead Gill, and branches in two. Both paths are cairned. It is the left hand branch you should follow. This crosses Spouthead Gill and pulls up to the top of the pass where is to be found a first aid box sited next to a large boulder. (3/4 miles)

4 From the first aid box a well worn path leads directly uphill to the summit of Great Gable. (3/4 mile)

(A short walk of a hundred yards or so due south-west from the summit of Gable will bring you to the Westmorland Cairn, so called as it was built by two brothers who had the surname Westmorland. The brothers built the cairn to mark the point which they considered to be the finest view point in the Lake District.)

5 From the summit of Great Gable follow a line of cairns leading in a north westerly direction towards Ennerdale. After a hundred yards or so there begins a rugged rocky descent to Beck Head the gap between Great Gable and Kirk Fell. (1/2 mile)

6 *(If you wish to complete the walk at this stage by descending back to Wasdale head directly for the valley in a southerly direction, in doing this you will soon locate a line of cairns which leads to the path which descends in to the valley reaching the path you began on at the foot of its descent. Otherwise....)* From Beck Head there is a very obvious path climbing up on to Kirk Fell. The path actually follows the remains of an old metal fence; now just a series of isolated metal posts. There are few of these posts on the ascent but there are a good many on the top of the fell, which is just as well for once on the top there is little trace of a path. The posts trace a line which crosses over the two tops of Kirk Fell and then descends steeply down the other side of the fell to Black Sail Pass, the gap between Kirk Fell and Pillar, where it joins an old packhorse path which crosses over the pass. (1 1/2 miles)

7 On reaching the packhorse route turn left and follow it down the Mosedale valley to Wasdale Head where you rejoin the valley road. Here turn right and follow the road back to the car park. (2 1/4 miles)

SCAFELL 3162 feet

Distance	9 miles
Total Feet of Ascent	3000 feet
Suggested Time	6 hours
Starting Point	Foot of Hard Knott Pass (NY 212 012)
Car Parking	Verge side parking is possible along the road leading to the foot of the pass.

This walk passes through the most mountainous scenery in Cumbria. The ascent route along the side of the river Esk is the finest ascent in the Lake District and possesses several entrancing revelations. Scafell though is no place for getting disorientated in misty conditions as it is bounded by some very precipitous cliffs; good navigational skills on this walk are therefore essential.

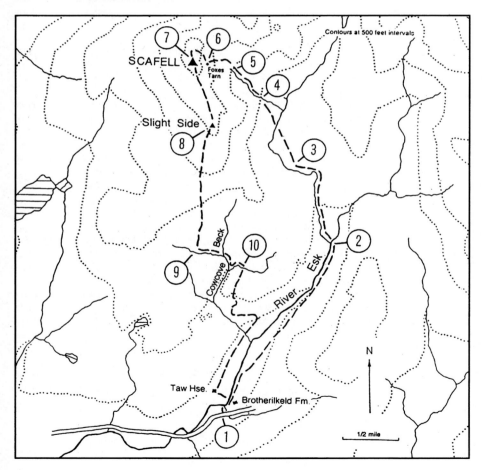

1 From the foot of Hard Knott Pass follow the access road leading to Brotherilkeld Farm. Before entering the farm a path branches off to the left following the edge of the river Esk. After passing through a gateway the path crosses two large fields and then continues along the edge of the river Esk again to a small packhorse bridge. (2 miles)

2 Crossing over the bridge the path continues to follow the river Esk but this time at a much steeper angle. Passing through a miniature gorge however the terrain dramatically levels again and the river takes a large curve westwards. The path continues along the side of the river following its westward course, but in little more than a quarter of a mile the course of the river alters yet again and a wide spacious valley comes in to view. (1 mile)

3 Immediately ahead of you is an extensive and impressive rock face called Cam Spout Crags. At the northern end of the crags is a waterfall, Cam Spout after which the crags are named. Follow a fairly distinctive path which heads to the base of this waterfall, fording the river Esk to do so. (3/4 mile)

4 To the right of the waterfall is a steep scramble. This is actually the start of a long, steep, path which leads to Mickledore, the gap between Scafell and Scafell Pike. Follow this route until you come to the start of a boulder field, 500 to 600 feet from the top of Mickledore itself. (3/4 mile)

5 After climbing roughly 200 feet from the start of the boulder field you should be able to observe to your left a deep narrow gully. Though something of a scramble this is the route to Foxes Tarn. You should find clear signs of usage as you climb it. (1/4 mile)

6 From Foxes Tarn the path continues up a scree slope to the summit ridge of Scafell. On reaching the top of this ridge turn left to reach the summit itself. (1/4 mile)

7 From the summit follow the summit ridge south to Slight Side. (1 mile)

8 Follow the cairned path which descends off Slight Side until you come to a swift flowing stream, the first real beck you come across on your descent, after descending some thirteen hundred feet. (3/4 mile)

9 Follow the beck downstream to its junction with Cowcove Beck. Then follow Cowcove Beck downstream a couple of hundred yards to where another tributary, Damas Dubs, flows in from the left. Now follow this tributary up stream a few hundred yards to a footbridge created out of two sheets of corrugated iron. (1/2 mile.)

10 Follow the path crossing the footbridge southwards. It is an old constructed pathway and descends gently to Taw House Farm. From the farm an enclosed footpath leads to a single beam footbridge crossing the river Esk and back to the walk's starting point. (1 1/2 miles)

SCAFELL PIKE 3207 feet

Distance	8 miles
Total Feet of Ascent	3500 feet
Suggested Time	6 hours
Starting Point	Wasdale Head car park (NY 187 087)

This is a walk to the highest point in England and therefore a very popular object. As a walk it certainly has a mountainous quality to it, but because of its over popularity it cannot be said to be the best summit to obtain in the Lake District. The route described here attempts to mitigate some of this problem in two ways. Firstly by choosing an ascent route via Lingmell; this is an infrequently trodden route yet it affords some very fine views of Mosedale and the Scafells. And secondly by descending from Sty Head via the old Borrowdale to Wasdale bridleway which is much easier under foot and much quieter than the main path to Wasdale and therefore well worth the effort of locating.

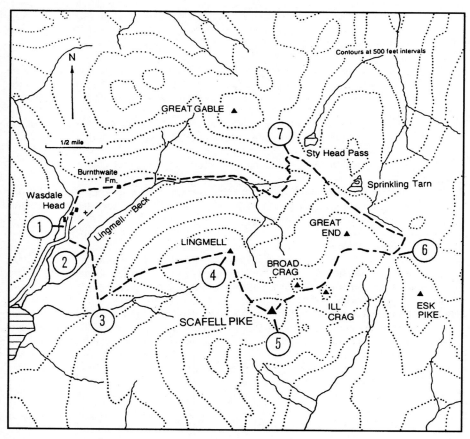

1 Walk south back along the valley road. Within two hundred yards along the road on the left hand side of the road, beginning from the same point, is the start of a public bridleway and a public footpath, both signposted with a metal signpost. Follow the public footpath, which is waymarked with a series of posts, by crossing the stile signed with the word 'Scafells'. The path leads to a footbridge spanning Lingmell Beck. (1/4 mile)

2 From the other side of the foot bridge a path climbs diagonally uphill to the right. The path levels when it reaches the crest of a ridge dotted with isolated hawthorn trees. It is important to notice here that the path crosses a much grassier path that follows the line of the ridge. This intersection the author has sought to indicate with the construction of a modest cairn. (1/2 mile)

3 Here turn left and begin the steep ascent of the ridge. As the steepness of the ridge lessens so does the distinctiveness of the path. When in any doubt always keep to the crest of the ridge. In this way eventually the top of Lingmell, marked with a large distinctive cairn, is reached. (1 1/4 mile)

4 From the top of Lingmell turn right following a distinct path down to Lingmell Col, the gap between Lingmell and Scafell Pike. As you reach the col the path disappears but a few hundred yards ahead, if there is no mist, you should observe a worn path climbing out of the valley to your right to the summit of the Scafell Pike. Join this path and follow it to the summit. (3/4 mile)

5 From the summit of Scafell Pike head north-east along a very worn rocky path. Initially the path descends steeply to Broad Crag Col and then climbs on to Broad Crag itself. From Broad Crag it dips down slightly and then crosses over Ill Crag to a shallow col between Ill Crag and Great End. Here the path swings right to Esk Hause, the broad deep gap between Great End and Esk Pike. On reaching the lowest point of this gap the path splits in two. (1 1/4 miles)

6 Follow the left hand branch. Within a few hundred yards, after passing a wind shelter and becoming reddish in colour, the path intersects with another path before climbing up hill. Here turn left and follow the new path towards Great Gable passing on the way Sprinkling Tarn. At the foot of Gable, at Sty Head Pass, next to a large boulder is located a first aid box. (1 1/2 miles)

7 From the first aid box a very distinct path heads in a westerly direction down to Wasdale. However if you veer left about 30 degrees from this path, in the direction of Broad Crag, within a hundred yards you should locate the semblance of a path that leads in to a small rock crevice. From here on the path is distinctive. It is in fact the old bridleway that crosses over Sty Head Pass from the head of Borrowdale to the head of Wasdale and is a more pleasing path to follow than the main path. On reaching Burnthwaite Farm the path branches in two. Either path leads back to the car park. The left hand path, which passes through the farm, is more direct, but again the less direct path, the right hand option, will prove more pleasing. (2 1/2 miles)

PILLAR 2927 feet

Distance	9 1/2 miles
Total Feet of Ascent	3300 feet
Suggested Time	6 1/2 hours
Starting Point	Overbeck Bridge (NY 168 068)
Car Parking	Adjacent to bridge

Beginning from Lakeland's most majestic valley this walk to the summit of Pillar is via the High Level Route, possibly the most adventurous mile of path in the Lake District. The path is ascribed to John Tyson Robinson an early rock climbing pioneer who developed the path as a way of reaching Pillar Rock which was then, and still is, a major rock climbing crag. Robinson's cairn was built in his memory. On reaching it Pillar Rock comes fully in to view.

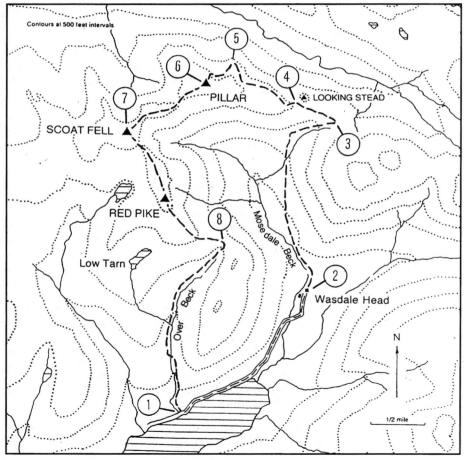

1   Follow the road to the Wasdale Head Inn at the valley head. (1 3/4 miles)

2   From behind the hotel continue along a path which follows Mosedale Beck. Do not cross the bridge which this path quickly comes to but continue along the eastern side of the beck. After passing through a five-bar gate the path follows the side of a wall in to Mosedale itself. This is an old packhorse route and gradually climbs to the top of Black Sail Pass. (2 miles)

3   On reaching the isolated remains of an old metal gate on top of the pass turn left following a path which initially follows a line of metal posts. This path leads to a small saddle between Looking Stead, a small rounded hillock to the right of the ridge, and the shoulder of Pillar itself. (1/2 mile)

4   From this saddle the path continues along the shoulder of Pillar. This is the easiest route to the top but a more exciting route is the High Level Route. To locate the somewhat elusive start of this route begin climbing the ridge but only a hundred feet or so. Look carefully at each cairn you come to. From one particular cairn, at the time of writing it is the second cairn, a narrow path leads off to the right. This is the start. To begin with the path descends slightly and then delicately traverses the northern face of Pillar to Robinson's Cairn, situated on top of a prominent knoll. Unfortunately in recent years a confusing alternative path has developed. About a hundred yards from the start the route now almost imperceptibly branches in two. Try to ensure that you spot this bifurcation and that you take the left hand, higher, path. This is the original and superior route. (3/4 mile)

5   From Robinson's Cairn the path is obvious enough even if the terrain seems daunting. The path descends at first and then ascends a scree slope at the top of which it moves right across a tilted slab, called the Shamrock Traverse, bringing you to a point overlooking Pillar Rock. From here the path ascends a steep ridge to the summit of Pillar. (1/2 mile)

6   From the summit head S.W. down to Wind Gap and then along the ridge to Scoat Fell the summit cairn of which is a small pile of stones set on top of a stone wall. (3/4 mile)

7   From Scoat Fell head S.E. to the top of Red Pike. Initially there is no path but a few isolated cairns pick out the route across a boulder strewn surface. From Red Pike a distinct path descends to Dore Head. (1 1/2 miles)

8   From Dore Head move S.W. in to the Over Beck valley, keeping to the western side of the stream. Despite there being a public right of way marked on the map there is little evidence of a path on the ground. It is a soggy plod until you reach the stream flowing from Low Tarn where a constructed pathway is to be found. You now seem assured of an easy path, but not so. The path leads to a wall through which there is no right of way. Follow the wall downhill to a footbridge crossing Over Beck. The path leading from it on the other side is obvious but narrow and follows the final section of the river back to the car park. (2 miles)

THE BUTTERMERE FELLS

Highest Point	High Stile 2644 feet
Distance	10 miles
Total Feet of Ascent	3100 feet
Suggested Time	6 1/2 hours
Starting Point	Buttermere Village Car Park (NY 175 169)

The Buttermere Fells, Red pike, High Stile and High Crag form one of the finest ridge walks in the Lake District. The approach taken in this walk via Scale Force is not as steep or as arduous as the more direct route from Buttermere via Bleaberry Tarn, nor is it as busy. After the ridge proper, and the descent to Scarth Gap, the pull up to Hay Stacks is arduous but totally rewarding. The final miles of the walk follow the peaceful shores of Buttermere lake, from which you can look up and admire those fells over which you were crossing but a few hours before.

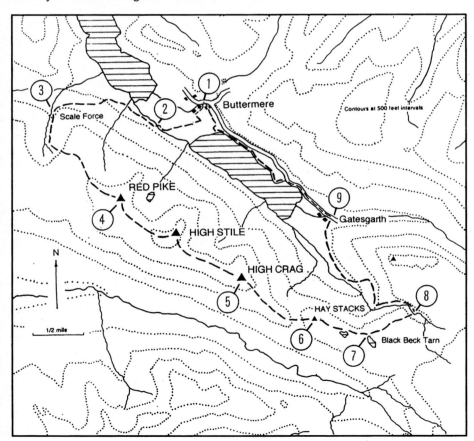

1   From the Buttermere village follow an obvious trackway to the left of the Fish Hotel signposted as leading to Buttermere Lake and Scale Bridge for roughly one hundred yards until you come to a kissing gate at a bend in the trackway. Pass through the gate and proceed along the trackway it gives access to Scale Bridge. (1/2 mile)

2   Cross over the bridge and turn right following a path leading north-westwards. Initially the path seems to be heading to Crummock Water but in fact veers away from the lake towards the gap between Melbreak and Red Pike where it comes to the foot of Scale Force, the longest waterfall in the Lake District, recessed in a deep ravine. (1 1/4 mile)

3   Just before coming to the foot of the ravine a reddish path, partially cobble to begin with, climbs steeply uphill to the left. This path leads to the top of the falls where it follows Scale Beck, the stream which forms the falls. A path soon veers off to the left from this path but be sure to ignore it. Coming to a tributary of Stake Beck the path itself veers uphill to the left eventually reaching Lingcomb Edge which it then follows to the summit of Red Pike. (1 1/2 miles)

4   Continue along the summit ridge from Red Pike on to High Stile and then on to High Crag. (1 1/2 miles)

5   From High Crag there is as steep descent to Scarth Gap followed by a steep climb to the top of Hay Stacks. (1 mile)

6   From the top of Haystacks the ridge path continues eastwards to a sizable tarn known as Innominate Tarn and then makes a short rocky descent to a second tarn called Blackbeck Tarn. (1/2 mile)

7   Here the path crosses over the outflow of Blackbeck Tarn and strikes out in a slightly different direction, north-easterly, weaving around some attractive knolls and crags and finally descending down to a a distinctive beck flowing towards Buttermere; Warnscale Beck. (1/2 mile)

8   Cross over the beck and follow the path immediately to your left that contours above the stream to link up with a constructed path leading westwards down in to the valley which was originally built to transport slate from Dubs Quarry. Follow this path down to the roadway at Gatesgarth. (1 1/2 miles)

9   Continue along the road to where it meets the lakeshore of Buttermere lake. From this point a signposted path follows the lakeshore back to Buttermere village, which has one pleasantly surprising feature that no other path in Lakeland has and which the author leaves the reader to discover. (1 3/4 miles)

WALKS LOCATION MAP

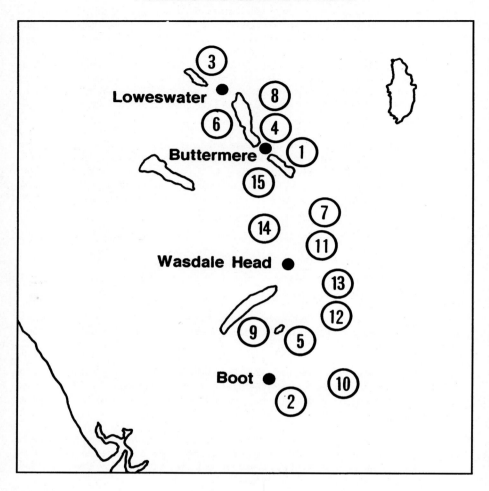